THE NORMANS

Peter Chrisp

Thomson Learning

New York

Look into the Past

First published in the
United States in 1995 by
Thomson Learning
115 Fifth Avenue
New York, NY 10003

First published in 1994 by Wayland (Publishers) Ltd.

Library of Congress Cataloging-in-Publication Data
Chrisp, Peter.
  The Normans / Peter Chrisp
          p.   cm. — (Look into the past)
  Includes bibliographical references and index.
  ISBN 1-56847-174-2
  1. Normans — France — Normandy — Juvenile literature.
2. Normandy (France) — History —To 1515 — Juvenile
literature. 3. Normandy, Dukes of — Juvenile literature.
4. Normans — England — Juvenile literature. 5. Normans
—Mediterranean Region — Juvenile literature.
[1. Normans.] I. Title. II. Series.
DC611.N856   1995
940'.04395 — dc20   94-31059

Printed Italy

Picture acknowledgments

The publishers wish to thank the following for providing the
photographs in this book: British Museum 19; C. M. Dixon
22 (bottom), 24 (bottom), 27, 28, 29; E. T. Archive 7,
18 (top), 21, 23; Werner Forman Archive 5; Michael Holford
6, 8, 9, 10, 11, 12, 13, 14, 15, 17, 19 (top and middle), 20,
24 (top); Topham 16, 22 (top), 25.
Map artwork by Jenny Hughes.
Artwork on page 18 by Stephen Wheele.

CONTENTS

Words that appear in **bold italic** in the text are explained in the glossary on page 30.

WHO WERE THE NORMANS?

The Normans were a warlike people from Normandy, a small area on the north coast of France. They are famous today for the conquests they made between 1030 and 1150, which are shown on the map below. The best known conquest was that of England in 1066, but Norman knights also conquered southern Italy, Sicily, Malta, Antioch in the *Middle East,* and part of north Africa. They also tried, but failed, to conquer Greece. In the 1170s a French poet named Jordan Fantosme summed up the Normans in these words: "The Normans are good conquerors. There is no race like them."

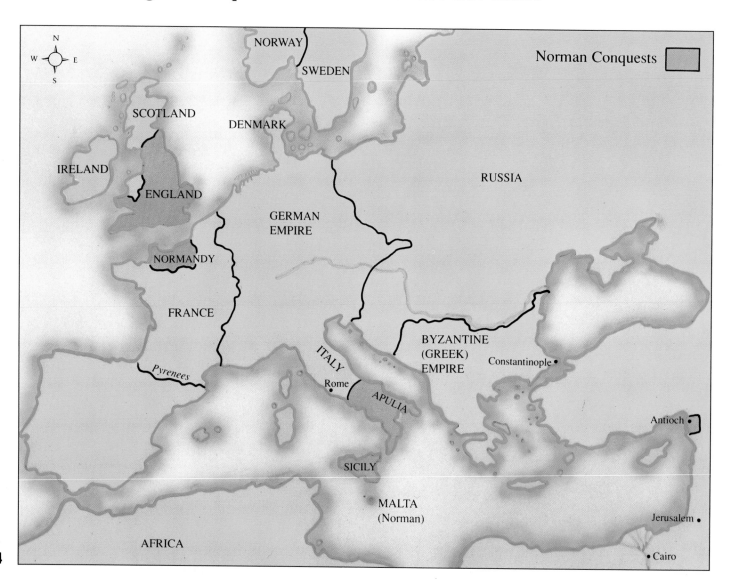

In the beginning, the Normans were known as **Vikings**. The word *Norman* means "north man," or Viking. The Vikings were fierce raiders from Norway, Sweden, and Denmark. They attacked the coasts of western Europe in their longships. A Viking longship is carved on this stone from Sweden.

In the year 911, the French king, Charles the Simple, allowed a Viking raider named Rolf (or Rollo) to settle on the north coast of France. Charles's plan was that Rolf would defend the coast against other Vikings. The arrangement was very successful.

Rolf and his fellow Vikings eventually gave up their old religion and became Christians. They married French women and settled down.

Within a hundred years, the Viking settlers were speaking French. The part of France they settled came to be called "Normandy," the land of the north men. The Vikings had become the Normans.

KNIGHTS AND HORSES

The Normans were able to win many battles, thanks to their skill at fighting on horseback. From the age of seven or eight, the sons of Norman nobles learned to ride and fight. Their war horses, called destriers, were bred to be fast and strong and were trained not to panic in battle. A good war horse was very expensive.

◄ Here, Norman knights are charging into battle on their war horses. They wear small helmets with nose guards and heavy suits of chain mail (armor made from hundreds of tiny metal rings). They carry long, kite-shaped shields and light lances, used for jabbing or throwing.

◄ These two knights are using a heavier type of lance. It was gripped tightly under the arm and used like a battering ram to knock over the enemy. These pictures come from the Bayeux Tapestry, an embroidery nearly 200 feet long that shows the Norman conquest of England in 1066.

This Norman knight riding a stocky horse is a chess piece from southern Italy, another place conquered by the Normans. The knight carries a long, slashing sword, used when the lance had been broken or thrown. Chess, a game about war, was very popular with the Normans.

7

1066: THE CONQUEST OF ENGLAND

In the 1060s England was ruled by an old king named Edward the Confessor. Edward had no sons of his own to succeed him as king. William of Normandy, who was distantly related to Edward, felt that he had a strong claim to the throne. Another possible king was Harold Godwinson, the most powerful nobleman in England. These pictures, from the Bayeux Tapestry, show the struggle between Harold and William for the crown of England.

◀ At first Harold and William were friends. In 1064 or 1065, Harold sailed to Normandy and stayed with William. According to Norman writers, he swore to help William become king. Here Harold is swearing his oath in front of William.

◀ In 1066 King Edward of England died. On the left, English nobles are offering the crown to Harold. On the right, Harold sits on the throne, wearing his new crown.

William was furious. He quickly made plans to invade England and seize the throne. Here, carpenters cut wood and build ships for the invasion fleet. ▶

The ships are loaded with weapons, heavy suits of chain mail, and barrels of wine. ▼

Now the fleet, packed with horses and knights, sails for England. William's ship has a lantern on top of the mast. This was lit to keep the fleet together – the crossing took place at night, on September 27, 1066. ▼

11

While the Normans were crossing the sea, Harold was busy in the north of England. He was fighting another invading army, from Norway. Harold won that battle and then raced south to fight William. Their armies met near Hastings on October 14, 1066. In these scenes, the Norman knights are fighting on horseback, while the English fight on foot. They stand in a tight row called a "shield wall," armed with battle axes and spears. ▶

◀ The fighting lasted eight hours. This section shows how it ended. The writing says, "Here King Harold was killed." He may be the figure pulling an arrow from his eye, or he may be the man falling beneath the horse. Perhaps both figures show Harold at different stages of his last desperate fight.

With their king dead, the English army broke up and fled. In the lower border of the tapestry, the dead and dying English are being stripped of their armor. William had earned a new nickname, "the Conqueror."

The Norman conquest was the last successful invasion of England.

13

CASTLES

Although the Normans had beaten the English in battle, they did not feel safe. They knew that the English hated them and might attack at any time. Between 1067 and 1071, William's army had to fight to put down several uprisings by the English nobles. To protect themselves, and to make it easier to rule their new lands, the Normans built castles. Before 1066, these were almost unknown in England. Soon there were hundreds of them. "They filled the whole land with these castles," wrote an English monk in the 1130s, "and when these castles were built, they filled them with devils and wicked men."

Here is a famous Norman castle. It is called Falaise Castle, and is the place where William the Conqueror was born.

Early Norman ▶ castles were made from wood, which could easily catch fire. This picture shows the Normans attacking the castle of Dinan in Brittany. Two Norman knights are holding flaming torches up to the wooden walls. The Duke of Brittany is forced to surrender. He is handing over the castle keys on the end of a lance.

◀ In time the Normans replaced their wooden castles with stronger ones made of stone. Stonemasons from Normandy did the skilled work, while most of the laboring was done by English people. This is Rochester Castle in Kent, built around 1130. The tall building in the center is called a "keep." It is over 110 feet high and its walls are nearly 12 feet thick.

HUNTING AND FEASTING

When they were not fighting, Norman nobles loved to hunt wild animals. In those days the forests of England were full of deer and boar (wild pigs). The Normans chased them on horseback with packs of dogs. Then they killed them with their spears or with bows and arrows. This was a useful way of keeping both men and horses well trained for warfare. It was also a way of getting food, for the animals were cooked and eaten at great feasts after the day's hunting. Only the nobles were allowed to hunt these animals. If ordinary people were caught hunting, they could be killed.

▼ Some nobles are hunting with their dogs and a trained hawk. This is Harold with his friends before the conquest of England. They are easily recognizable as Anglo-Saxons because they have mustaches and their hair is longer than the Normans' hair. Saxon nobles liked to hunt as much as the Normans, but few of them got the chance after 1066. Most of those who were not killed in battle fled abroad.

This scene shows a feast being prepared. On ▶ the left, meat is being boiled in a pot. The man in the middle is picking up hot bread or cakes using tongs. Joints of meat have been roasted on spits, like kabobs.

▼ One of these men is blowing a horn. He is letting everyone know that the feast is ready. On the right, William and his barons are eating with knives and with their fingers; forks had not been invented. Bishop Odo, William's half brother, is blessing the meal.

LIFE ON THE LAND

Knights and barons made up only a tiny part of the population. Most people in Norman times farmed the land. Thanks to the hard work of these people, the nobles could spend their time hunting and fighting.

 The farming people belonged to different classes, depending upon how much land they held. For example, villeins were farmers who had more than thirty acres of land. Cottars had less than five acres. The lowest class of people were serfs, or slaves. They had no land at all and were treated as their lord's property.

We know about different classes of people ▶ because of the ***Domesday Book***. This is a great survey of the land ordered by William in 1086. He wanted to find out everything he could about England. In particular, he wanted to know how rich his kingdom was. The Domesday Book tells us the names of people who held land throughout the kingdom. It also records the amount of land they held and what they paid in taxes to the king. Even their farm animals were counted.

◀ Each village was surrounded by three huge fields, each divided into strips. Every year, two of the fields were planted with wheat, oats, or barley, while the third field was left ***fallow***. People had strips spread out among the three fields.

The borders of the Bayeux Tapestry show us the farmwork of ordinary people. The different stages in planting crops are shown here.

On the left, a donkey is being used to pull a plow. On the right, a man is sowing seed by scattering it over the plowed field. ▼

After sowing, the seed is covered over using a harrow (a spiked frame) pulled by a horse. ▶

◀ This picture comes from an English calendar painted thirty years before the Norman conquest. It shows the work that follows the harvesting of a crop such as wheat or barley. The crop is being beaten with sticks to separate the grains from the chaff (the unwanted stalks and husks). It is then tossed in the air. The chaff blows away while the heavier grains fall to the ground. It was hard work being a farmer.

19

RELIGION

The Normans were Christians, people who worship Jesus Christ. As Christians, they believed that after death everyone was judged by Christ. People who had followed the rules of the Christian religion were rewarded in heaven. Everyone else suffered in hell. This reward or punishment lasted forever.

▲ The teachings of Christianity are in a book called the Bible. However, in Norman times, few people could read, and most did not know Latin, the language in which their version of the Bible was written. Many people learned about Christianity from the paintings that covered the walls of every church. This painting, from Chaldon in Surrey, shows wicked people tumbling down to hell where they are tortured by devils. Meanwhile, good people, helped by angels, climb a ladder up into heaven.

▲ When people went to worship in the
Norman *cathedral* of Monreale in Sicily, they
could see a huge figure of Jesus Christ above
their heads. His head and shoulders alone are
54 feet high. This is a mosaic, a picture made
from thousands of tiny colored tiles. The
Normans could never forget that Jesus was
watching and judging them.

The **Church** ►
taught that there were various ways that people could avoid going to hell. To start with, they could be baptized – blessed with holy water from a font, or basin. This Norman font from Winchester shows Saint Nicholas helping a poor man and his three daughters. Saints were people who had led holy lives. Norman Christians often prayed to saints.

Knights believed they had their own way of getting to heaven: going on a *crusade*. A crusade was a holy war fought to free the "holy land" from non-Christians, especially from *Muslims*. The most successful was the First Crusade (1096-99), which ended in the capture of Jerusalem. Among its leaders were two famous Normans, Robert Curthose, son of William the Conqueror, and Bohemond "the Giant," a leader of the Normans in Italy. Bohemond made himself ruler of Antioch (see map on page 4).

Jerusalem, the city where Christ died and was buried, was seen by Christians as the holiest place on earth. This is a map of the world, watched over by Christ. Jerusalem is in the middle. Christians believed that Jerusalem was the center of the world. ▼

◄ Another way of serving Christ was to become a *monk* or a *nun*. These were men and women who lived apart from ordinary people in monasteries and nunneries. They spent their days in prayer. This is the storehouse of Fountains Abbey, a monastery in Yorkshire. The king and his nobles paid for the building of monasteries. This was their way of serving Christ. They also hoped that the prayers of the monks and nuns would help them get to heaven.

23

In Norman times, men who had joined the ▶ Church as priests or monks were easy to recognize; they shaved the tops of their heads. This man's rich robes are a sign that he is not just an ordinary priest. He is a **bishop**, one of the important leaders of the Church. Norman bishops were also barons. They had their own castles and knights who fought for them.

The church where a bishop had his headquarters was called a cathedral. This was because the bishop had his cathedra, or seat, there. Cathedrals were the biggest structures that the Normans built. They spent huge sums of money on them to show their love of God.

◀ This is Durham Cathedral, which towers over the city. It must have been even more impressive in Norman times, when most people lived in small wooden houses.

There were ▶
Anglo-Saxon
cathedrals before
1066, but they were
much smaller than
those built by the
Normans. This was
because the Anglo-
Saxons were not as
good at building with
stone. This picture
shows how skilled the
Norman builders
were. This is the
inside of Winchester
Cathedral, built on
William the
Conqueror's orders. If
you visit a cathedral
in Europe, look for
round arches like
these. They were built
by the Normans.

THE NORMANS IN THE SOUTH

In Norman times, Italy was not a single country. The north was part of the Holy Roman (or German) *Empire*. The southernmost area was ruled by Byzantine Greeks. In between, there were several states ruled by the Pope and by a people called the Lombards. The island of Sicily was ruled by Muslim Arabs. These different peoples were often at war with each other and they were always ready to hire foreigners to do their fighting for them. Italy was the perfect place for Norman knights to go to make their fortune.

◄ The most successful knights were Robert Guiscard ("The Crafty") and his younger brother Roger. By 1059, the two of them had conquered Apulia and Calabria, which Robert ruled as duke. It was his son Bohemond who went off on the First Crusade (see page 23). Meanwhile, in 1061, Roger crossed the sea to Sicily and began a war against the Muslims. By 1071, he was ruling most of the island from his capital, Palermo. In 1130 all the conquests in Italy were joined together into a single kingdom. It was ruled by Roger's son, who called himself King Roger II.

This mosaic shows ▶ King Roger II of Sicily being crowned by Christ. Roger was a successful conqueror, adding Malta and part of Africa to his kingdom. Unlike most Norman rulers, he was also well educated and could speak Latin, Greek, and Arabic as well as French. In this mosaic Roger is dressed just like Greek emperors of the time. He looks very different from the short-haired Normans of the Bayeux Tapestry.

▲ In Sicily, the Normans ruled over a mixed people including many Muslims and Greeks. As a result, the churches of Norman Sicily show a mixture of styles.

This is part of a Norman monastery at Palermo. It is the cloister, the place where the monks walked. It looks nothing like any of the cloisters that Normans built in northern Europe. The delicate columns, the rich patterns, and the fountain in the foreground were all features of Muslim palaces.

◀ Only by looking closely at the columns of the monastery at Palermo can one see a clue that this was the work of Normans. There are two figures who stand guard on top of this column. They are Norman knights.

INDEX